ELIZABETH RING

COMPANION DOGS

MORE THAN BEST FRIENDS

GOOD DOGS!
THE MILLBROOK PRESS · BROOKFIELD, CONNECTICUT

FOR JOAN,
GOOD BUDDY!

Cover photograph courtesy of Don D'Angelo

Photographs courtesy of Wide World Photos: pp. 3, 17, 26;
Bill Hennefrund: pp. 4, 11, 15, 20, 22; The Quaker Oats
Company: p. 7; Kent and Donna Dannen: pp. 9, 13;
Doug Heppner: p. 19; St. Hubert's Giralda: p. 25;
Illustration on p. 8 by Anne Canevari Green

Library of Congress Cataloging-in-Publication Data

Ring. Elizabeth, 1920-
Companion dogs: more than best friends / by Elizabeth Ring.
p. cm. — (Good dogs!)
Includes bibliographical references and index.
Summary: Describes training for companion dogs and therapeutic
dogs, including some dogs who have performed heroic rescues.
ISBN 1-56294-293-X (lib. bdg.)
1. Dogs—Social aspects—Juvenile literature. 2. Dogs
Therapeutic use—Juvenile literature. 3. Dogs—Training—Juvenile
literature. 4. Human-animal relationships—Juvenile literature.
5. Animal heroes—Juvenile literature. [1. Dogs—Training.
2. Human-animal relationships.] I. Title. II. Series.
SF426.5.R57 1994
636.7—dc20   93-15661 CIP AC

Published by The Millbrook Press
2 Old New Milford Road
Brookfield, Connecticut 06804

COMPANION DOGS

A dog's
love and
loyalty
make it a
perfect
companion.

One sunny spring morning in Livingston, Montana, Kenny Homme asked his mother if he could go outside and water the garden.

"Sure," she said. "Just stay in the yard, okay?"

"Okay," Kenny said. Although he was only five years old, he was pretty good about minding his mom.

He called to his dog, a Chesapeake Bay retriever and Kenny's best friend. "Come on, Chessie. Let's go!"

Chester was out the back door as soon as Kenny opened it. He rolled on the lawn while Kenny turned on the garden hose. Kenny carefully watered the plants that were just poking their green heads out of the ground. Then Kenny aimed the hose at the dog. Chester leaped in the air, snapping at the stream of water. Chester loved playing in the water.

When Kenny turned off the hose, he noticed the sound of the creek, close by. It was rumbling louder than he had ever heard it before. Forgetting his promise to stay close to the house, he wandered over to find out why the creek was so noisy.

From where he stood at the top of the steep bank, Kenny could see that the rushing water was much higher than usual. He leaned forward, trying to see how deep the stream was. Suddenly, his foot slipped and he tumbled down the muddy bank into the torrent. Immediately, the swift current caught him up and carried him downstream.

"Help!" he yelled. "Help me-e-e-e!"

Chester barked and leaped into the water after Kenny.

Kenny's mother, who had been checking on her son from time to time from the kitchen window, heard Kenny's shout. She rushed toward the creek just in time to see Chester reach Kenny's side. In horror, she watched as both Kenny and Chester were swept away. As fast as she could, she raced after them along the edge of the creek, but the boy and the dog were way ahead of her.

Kenny grabbed for Chester's hair, but he lost his grip. Choking, he clutched at Chester again, but the dog slipped through his hands. Then, just as the water carried them into a tunnel, he made one more grab. This time he caught hold.

With Kenny clinging to his back, Chester swam out of the tunnel. He pulled Kenny to the bank, and the two of them scrambled to safety.

That year, when Chester was named the Ken-L Ration "Dog Hero of the Year," he had no idea what all the fuss was about. But to the Homme family, Chester was the bravest of heroes.

"If we didn't have Chester," Mrs. Homme said at the time, "we wouldn't have a son right now."

Kenny and Chester shared many good times together after that day, closer friends than ever before.

Dogs in Human History · Dogs and people have been companions for thousands of years. Over the centuries, different breeds have been developed from the animals that first lived with cavemen. As years went by, the dogs changed in many ways.

Kenny Homme owes his life to his best friend, Chester. Here they pose happily after Chester rescued Kenny from drowning and became a hero.

Dogs belong to the same family of mammals as wolves, jackals, coyotes, and foxes. This early wild dog looks most like a jackal.

Some dogs (such as Siberian huskies) took on a wolflike appearance. But others looked nothing like wolves (the most likely ancestor of dogs). Some looked like jackals (another possible dog ancestor) or even like coyotes or foxes (other members of the canine family). Other breeds looked completely different—although you would never mistake a dog for a cat or a ferret or any other kind of animal.

In time, through selective breeding, people created short-legged dogs (like dachshunds) and bow-legged dogs (like bull-dogs) and long-legged dogs (like greyhounds). Some dogs (such as pugs) were bred to have flat faces and short noses. In other dogs (such as bloodhounds) long, floppy ears were encouraged. In still other dogs (such as schnauzers) ears perked up, straight and stiff. Ears of other dogs (such as collies) stood up but bent at the tips. Different dogs developed different coats: long or short hair, thin or thick, curly or straight. Tails curled up and over dogs' backs or grew long and ropy.

Some breeds (such as German shepherds) became known for their intelligence, strength, and self-confidence; others (such as golden retrievers) were valued for their great gentleness and patience—as well as their aptitude for obedience.

Dogs come in many shapes and sizes. The one trait they all have in common is their ability—some would say yearning—to devote themselves to people.

People have bred dogs for their useful qualities. For instance, swift hunters have been mated with other swift hunters. Strong dogs (such as dogs used in the old days to pull peddlers' wagons or work treadmills) have been bred with other strong dogs. Careful breeding has also produced dogs that are very good at herding sheep, retrieving wild game, tracking people, or assisting people who are disabled.

Dogs have been bred to strengthen qualities such as calmness of disposition or eagerness to learn. Breeding also produces the good looks admired at dog shows (which might be called part canine beauty pageants and part canine testing grounds of the dogs' obedience skills).

Dogs and People Today · Today there are over four hundred different breeds of dogs. As dogs have become different from each other over the years, one thing has remained the same: their close link with people.

People sometimes feel that dogs are even better friends than people. A dog never picks on you, scolds you, or lies to you. A dog, in fact, never judges you at all. It never notices what you wear or how you cut your hair. Neither does it care how rich or poor you are, or what kind of grades you get in school.

There are dozens of stories of dogs' loyalty to people. Once a dog has attached itself to a person, it seems that almost nothing can break the bond.

One German shepherd dog refused to leave a Moscow airport after her owner left on a plane for Siberia, unable to take the dog with him. Every day for two years the dog ran to meet

Dogs believe themselves to be part of the family. No matter what you're doing or where you're going, all they ask is to be included.

planes. She would let no one approach her, and she ate only scraps of food. She seemed healthy enough and accustomed to her way of life. Finally, however, she allowed herself to be coaxed into a new home.

Brawny, a chocolate Labrador retriever, stayed for three freezing days in the Connecticut woods beside his companion, who had fallen. The dog's constant barking finally brought help. The man died from exposure, and Brawny's legs were paralyzed for a time. The veterinarian who treated the dog said he believed some canine instinct told Brawny to try to keep the man warm.

On another cold day in New York State, a little girl was lost on a mountainside. This story has a happy ending because her dog kept her warm until help came.

Many dog experts believe that a dog's sense of loyalty is in its blood. Devotion, they say, is a natural trait. Just as wild dogs are faithful to the members of their packs (especially to the pack's leader), so domestic dogs are faithful to their human families (especially to the person who feeds, trains, and spends the most time with them).

Dog Heroes · Many people believe that loyalty plays a big part in a dog's risking its life to save its companion. Can a dog be a hero? Was Kenny Homme's dog, Chester, truly brave in jumping into the stream after the boy, or was he playing a new water game with Kenny? Did he act by instinct, without thinking of any danger involved? Was it possible that some sixth sense told the dog that Kenny was in real danger? Or *what*?

There are awards for dogs who perform heroic acts and awards
for dogs who are simply polite. Here a proud owner shows off her
Samoyed's Canine Good Citizenship certificate.

Nobody knows just what goes on in a dog's mind. There are
many guesses, but even scientists who study animal behavior do
not agree on exactly why dogs do what they sometimes do.

Nevertheless, since 1954, the Quaker Oats Company (maker
of a variety of dog foods) has given awards to "dog heroes"
every year. Sometimes awards go to dogs that are trained to
guide blind people or help deaf or disabled people.

Other awards are given to dogs like Chester—companion dogs trained only to behave politely in human society. All the award winners have performed what appear to be "heroic acts."

Tang, a collie who won the first Quaker Oats Ken-L Ration dog-hero award, saved a two-year-old child from falling off a milk truck. He simply parked himself in front of the truck so it could not move, barking until the driver got out and discovered the little girl perched on the back of the truck.

Buddy, a young basset hound, rescued a man who was attacked by a 400-pound (180-kilogram) hog in a barnyard. Buddy's leg was broken in his fight with the hog, but the man escaped, unharmed.

Sheba, an Alaskan malamute, knocked down a two-year-old child and covered her with his body, protecting her from a swarm of yellow jackets. Sheba nearly died from the twenty-seven stings she received, but the child was stung only once.

Leo, a standard poodle, saved two children from a diamond-back rattlesnake by jumping between them and the snake. Leo was bitten six times and, like Sheba, almost died. But the children were not hurt at all.

Dogs have saved people from almost any danger you can think of: fires, earthquakes, drowning, gas fumes, burglars—to mention a few.

How Dogs and People Communicate · Communication takes many forms: language, body movements, facial expressions. All of these ways serve to make the bond between dogs and people strong and lasting.

Dogs can learn many human words. Some dogs that are trained to help disabled people are taught as many as sixty separate commands. Family dogs, too, learn the words used in training them to behave: "down," "sit," "stay," and many more.

Dogs pick up key words that we use with each other, such as "out," "car," "dinner," and the names of people in the family. Have you ever had to spell out a word (as in: "I think I'll go for a w-a-l-k") so your dog won't know what you are saying?

A little boy explains ball-playing rules to his pet. How much the dog really understands may never be known, but "sit," "play," "ball," and "fetch" are probably part of its vocabulary.

Dogs have many ways of speaking to us. Although they do not think or feel as we do, dogs can, most of the time, make their messages perfectly plain.

For one thing, dogs use their voices to express themselves. Like human voices, dogs' barks have different tones. Depending on what is going on, a dog's bark can mean "hello" or "watch out" or "help." A whine can mean "I'm scared" or "let me out of here." A howl can mean "I'm lonesome," "I'm hurt," or simply "I'm here." A growl can mean "who are you?" or "I'm getting angry." Sometimes dogs put two sounds together, like a growl/bark or a yelp/bark or a bark that ends in a howl. Many dogs make sounds deep in their throats, each sound having a different meaning. You really have to know your dog well to guess what it might be saying.

Dogs' faces wear expressions that are not hard to understand. An angry dog may stare or glare at someone, often with ears flat against its head and teeth bared. A dog that has been punished is apt to hang its head and look up at you anxiously. A dog that keeps licking its lips may mean it is nervous and would rather not be approached. A happy dog's eyes may sparkle, and its ears may twitch; some dogs even seem to smile.

Dogs' bodies tell us a lot, too—especially a dog's tail. A tail held out straight and wagging hard may be saying the dog is wildly excited or is just feeling friendly. It might also mean the dog is asking for food, a pat, or a walk outside. Wagging slowly, it may mean the dog is asking a question, such as: "Are we going for a walk?" or "What's that you said?"

Body language and even facial expressions reveal everything this dog-walker needs to know about how his charges are feeling.

A tail held high with a fast, slight wag can mean the dog is anxious and tense. A high tail wagging fast and hard may mean the dog is ready for a fight. A tail tucked tight between a dog's hind legs usually shows fear.

Dogs often use their whole bodies to get their messages across to us. How would you read these canine signals?

• The dog bounds toward you, bows at your feet with its rear high, turns and runs off, then does it all over again. (Is it saying "Let's play!"?)

· The dog crawls toward you, lies down, and lifts its paw. (Is it saying "I'm sorry."?)

· The dog rolls on its back, waves its paws in the air, grunts and wriggles. (Is it saying "Wow! Am I glad to see you!"?)

The better you know your dog, the better you can guess what its messages mean.

A dog can read a great many of people's wordless messages. If, for instance, you put your coat on, the dog is apt to run toward the door, ready to go out before you are. If you dance across the living room, your dog is likely to wag its tail and prance along-side you, getting right into your happy mood.

Dogs that are trained to help people are taught to pay extra attention to their partners' movements. Asia, a service dog who lived with Dolores Justus of Wellsville, Kansas, was trained to assist her disabled friend in and out of bed, fetch the phone to her, and perform many other duties. But she did much more.

"Asia reads my body language and my moods," Dolores once said. "She watches me. She knows what is going on with me—even at night when I am asleep. When I have a nightmare, she wakes me up and comforts me. She is always there for me."

Since people are very different from one another and lead very different lives, it is fortunate that dogs, whether family companions or trained helpers, are extremely adaptable.

A perfect match. The bond between a dog and its companion
can bring a lifetime of happiness to each of them.

This does not mean that any dog can get along perfectly
with any person. A large rambunctious dog and a small quiet
person are not the best mix. A shy, nervous dog is probably not
going to enjoy a large noisy family. A jogger fits best with a dog
that loves to run. An office worker who has to leave a dog home
alone all day needs a dog that does not demand lots of exercise.

· 19 ·

Companion-Dog Training · Since dogs are so adaptable and have adopted us so wholeheartedly, one of the best things we can do for our dogs is to train them to be good citizens. Because a dog is anxious to please, it is only fair to let it know exactly what is expected of it. Training makes a dog feel confident, at ease in most human situations.

With patience and practice, you can easily train your dog to obey simple commands such as "stay." A well-trained dog is not only happy, it is safe.

A well-trained dog comes when you call it, stands still when you tell it to, waits quietly when it is left alone, knows better than to beg at the table, sleep on the couch, jump on guests, chew up the rug, or make puddles on the floor.

Every family has its own life-style, and a dog needs to know the meaning of "okay" and "no." Training is most successful with a lot of "okays" (which tell the dog "well done; your work is over"), many pats, and much praise. The less the word "no" is used, the better. (Brian Kilcommons, a well-known dog trainer, once half-jokingly said that most of the dogs in the United States grow up thinking their name is "No.")

Actually, a dog quickly learns its own name. It also quickly gets used to a collar and leash. Leashes are especially useful in teaching a dog to "come" and to "heel" (that is, to walk at your left side at the same pace you are walking).

Many pups start "puppy kindergarten" when they are between two and three months old, learning a few basic commands and "socializing," getting used to being with other people and dogs. Other pups start serious training when they are between four and six months old. Besides the usual lessons in manners, dogs can be trained to do almost anything that fits into a family's activities: fetch balls, pull a cart, carry a newspaper, jump over hurdles, or catch Frisbees on the fly.

Many people train their dogs to be watchdogs. That does not mean the dog is taught to attack strangers or bark at every sound out in the street. A good watchdog simply guards its property and barks at noises close to the house. Barking at strangers

Jogging is twice as much fun when a dog trots along
at your side. It's great exercise for the dog, too.

comes naturally to most dogs. So does protecting its own territory. Even a miniature poodle will bark furiously at a great dane if the big dog dares to cross the little dog's property line.

Therapy Dogs · Of all the things that come naturally to dogs, nothing means more to many people than a dog's natural friendliness. Scientific tests show that people who live alone are less lonely when they have an agreeable, well-behaved dog. Nervous people are calmer. Shy people are more confident. Young people become more responsible. The list goes on and on.

Because animals seem to have this good effect on people, many dogs are employed in "community work." They are frequently taken to visit invalids and elderly people in their homes. Dogs also go into hospitals, nursing homes, prisons, centers for people who have emotional or mental problems, homes where people are recovering from drug or alcohol addiction, and other institutions where people need care. In some places, dogs are permanent residents.

Sometimes such dogs are called "therapy dogs." The dogs, it has been found, help people feel better about the way they think and feel about themselves and the world. Dogs sometimes help sick people feel healthier. Such "animal-assisted therapy" is often carried out by volunteers (breeders, for instance, who make visits with their own dogs), not paid workers.

A therapy dog can be any kind of dog of any age. Most therapy dogs are not specially trained, although some are registered as "therapy dogs." Sometimes "service dogs," fully trained to assist blind, deaf, and disabled people, are used—not for their service skills but simply for their cheerful company.

A friendly dog can make a big difference to people who are away from their homes, their families, and their friends. A dog's company can make a strange place feel more like home—whether or not a person has had a dog before.

A Pekingese named Ding-A-Ling had all the qualities that make a good therapy dog. She was gentle and lovable. She was curious and outgoing. She needed no special training to be well-behaved and sociable.

The tiny dog lived at St. Hubert's Giralda Animal Welfare and Education Center in Madison, New Jersey. As part of St. Hubert's education program, she visited schools, nursing homes, and other places, such as the Dog Museum of New York. Whoever held the easy-going little dog on a lap or looked into her lively eyes could easily understand how important her friendly work must be.

By the time she retired at age fourteen, after ten years of service, Ding-A-Ling had met at least 130,000 people—a huge record for any dog, let alone such a tiny one. In 1990 she was named the "National Therapy Dog of the Year" in a contest jointly run by the Delta Society and the American Animal Hospital Association.

Dogs that visit nursing homes and mental hospitals often make friends with people who seem out of touch with other people. One day, when a golden retriever named Bo visited patients at the Bridgeport (Connecticut) Hospital, he was taken up to a

Evelyn Kempler enjoys Ding-A-Ling's company at St. Hubert's Giralda Animal Welfare and Education Center.

man who sat slumped in a wheelchair. The man was staring blankly into space. No one had been able to get him interested in anything at all.

Bo sat beside the chair, waiting for the man to notice him. When the man did not even glance at him, Bo gently put a paw on the man's lap. After a long moment, the man turned to the dog. Slowly, he reached out to pat him. Next, the man started to

Tiffany, a Siberian husky, is a dog volunteer at Newington Children's Hospital in Newington, Connecticut. She visits the hospital once a week to cheer up young patients.

talk to him. Bo responded by nuzzling the man's hand. It was not long before the man was talking to other people about the dog. After a while he was talking about other things. Bo had renewed the man's interest in the world around him. Everyone was amazed at the change in the man.

An even more surprising thing happened when a whole group of dogs, trained by Support Dogs of St. Louis, Missouri, was taken one day to visit patients at a children's hospital. One seven-year-old girl named Bridgette sat in a wheelchair, her left hand and arm partly paralyzed. She had recently come out of a coma following a head injury and could speak only a few words.

When the dogs appeared Bridgette's eyes lit up. "Walk," she said, grabbing the leash attached to the harness of a German shepherd dog named Sass. The dog's handler pushed the little girl in her wheelchair through the hospital halls, guiding the dog by a second leash attached to Sass's collar.

At the end of the walk, Bridgette strung three words together: "Walk the dog." As the dogs were about to leave, a Support Dog handler had Sass hold out a paw to shake hands—on Bridgette's left side. Bridgette used her right hand to lift her partly paralyzed left arm, held the dog's paw in her left hand and said "How do you do." When asked if she wanted the dogs to come back another day, she said "YES" loud and clear and laughed hard.

The dogs did return, and within two weeks Bridgette was talking in full sentences. She even (with some assistance) got out of her wheelchair for the first time to walk Sass.

When dogs visit prisons, inmates welcome their open affection. A dog, of course, does not know that a prisoner has committed a crime. It asks no questions about a person's past. It simply makes friends.

It has been found that a dog's presence in prison can make prisoners feel less angry or less suspicious or less aggressive. It even makes them feel more friendly toward other inmates.

In several correctional institutions, inmates have been given the job of caring for a dog (perhaps even training it to become a service dog for disabled people). The care of a dog often gives the inmates a greater sense of responsibility than they have ever had before. They take great pride in watching their dog's progress—knowing that the dog's success is due to the trainer's careful work.

Every day, more and more therapy dogs are being employed at hospitals, nursing homes, prisons, and other institutions. The dogs often seem to make people feel more normal and more a part of the outside world. Perhaps most important is the way dogs bring a sense of love into troubled lives.

By simply being themselves—eager, loyal, intelligent, and friendly—companion and therapy dogs often perform what might be called miracles. Maybe when a dog does something "heroic" it is just doing what comes naturally—only doing it a little bit better than usual.

FURTHER READING

Arneson, D. J. *A Friend Indeed.* New York: Franklin Watts, 1981.

Benjamin, Carol Lea. *Dog Training for Kids.* New York: Howell Book House, 1979.

Hancock, Judith M. *Friendship, You and Your Dog.* New York: Dutton, 1986.

McPherson, Mark. *Caring for Your Dog.* Mahwah, N. J.: Troll Associates, 1985.

Newman, Matthew. *Watch Guard Dogs.* New York: Macmillan, 1985.

Pope, Joyce. *Taking Care of Your Dog.* New York: Franklin Watts, 1990.

Squire, Ann. *Understanding Man's Best Friend: Why Dogs Look and Act the Way They Do.* New York: Macmillan, 1991.

INDEX

ABOUT THE AUTHOR

Free-lance writer and editor Elizabeth Ring is a former teacher and an editor at *Ranger Rick's Nature Magazine*. Her previous books for children include two biographies, *Rachel Carson: Caring for the Earth* and *Henry David Thoreau: In Step with Nature*, published by The Millbrook Press. Also published by The Millbrook Press are two other books by Elizabeth Ring in the *Good Dogs!* series, *Detector Dogs: Hot on the Scent* and *Assistance Dogs: In Special Service*. She has also written on a range of programs on environmental subjects for the National Wildlife Federation. She lives in Woodbury, Connecticut, with her husband, writer and photographer William Hennefrund. Although five dogs have been a part of the family over the years, three cats are current companions.